Leaping Lengths!

Relate Addition and Subtraction to Length

Eric Thanner

INFOMAX
MATH READERS

Rosen Classroom™

New York

Published in 2015 by The Rosen Publishing Group, Inc.
29 East 21st Street, New York, NY 10010

Copyright © 2015 by The Rosen Publishing Group, Inc.

All rights reserved. No part of this book may be reproduced in any form without permission in writing from the publisher, except by a reviewer.

Book Design: Katelyn Londino

Photo Credits: Cover Jeannette Katzir Photog/Shutterstock.com; p. 5 Michelle Sole/Shutterstock.com; p. 7 Cat Downie/Shutterstock.com; p. 9 Sue Robinson/Shutterstock.com; pp. 11, 13 (froghopper) Arto Hakola/Shutterstock.com; p. 13 (flea) Cosmin Manci/Shutterstock.com; p. 15 Stayer/Shutterstock.com; p. 17 Daniel J. Cox/The Image Bank/Getty Images; p. 19 Neil Burton/Shutterstock.com; p. 21 Christopher Meder/Shutterstock.com; p. 22 photobar/Shutterstock.com.

ISBN: 978-1-4777-4760-5
6-pack ISBN: 978-1-4777-4764-3

Manufactured in the United States of America

CPSIA Compliance Information: Batch #WS15RC: For further information contact Rosen Publishing, New York, New York at 1-800-237-9932.

Contents

Animals on the Move	4
What Is a Number Line?	6
The World's Best Jumpers	8
Jumping Cats	14
Who Else Jumps?	18
Measuring Movements	22
Glossary	23
Index	24

Animals on the Move

The animals in our world live in many different **environments**. Over time, their bodies have **adapted** to help them move in their environments in the best way possible.

Many animals have body parts that help them swim, crawl, fly, or climb. Some animals have body parts that help them jump. They jump from place to place in search of food, water, and a safe home.

Can you think of some animals that jump?

5

What Is a Number Line?

Animals that jump can be big or small. Depending on their size, their jumps are big or small, too. We can use measuring tools such as rulers and meter sticks to measure a jump's length and **distance**. Number lines are like these measuring tools. You can use a number line to help you add or subtract the length of animals' jumps. It makes math easy!

> This number line shows inches. Other number lines may show feet, meters, or centimeters. No matter what **unit** of measurement it shows, a number line's spaces are always equal.

0 1 2 3 4 5 6
inches

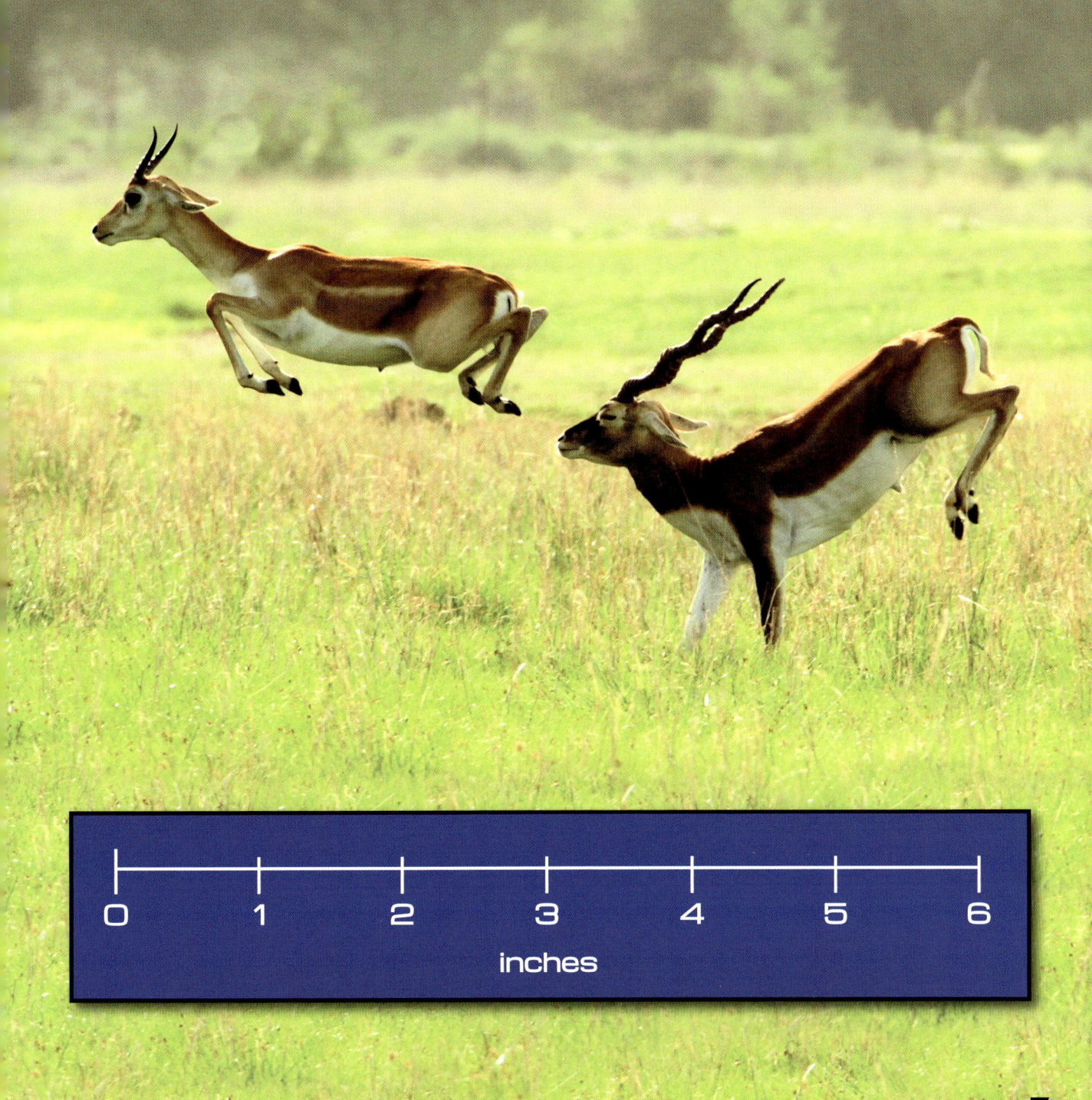

7

The World's Best Jumpers

The froghopper is a bug that's an excellent jumper. The length of its jumps compared to its small size makes it the best jumper in the world.

A froghopper jumps 7 inches to reach a nearby plant. Then it jumps to another plant, which is 8 inches away. How long are the 2 jumps altogether? Use a number line to help you add.

> The first jump measures 7 inches, so draw a line to the 7-inch mark. To draw the line for the second jump, count 8 more marks to the right. That brings you to the 15-inch mark.

7 inches
+ 8 inches
―――――――
15 inches

first jump   second jump
0 1 2 3 4 5 6 7 8 9 10 11 12 13 14 15
inches

9

The froghopper lands on top of a plant that's 14 inches tall. It has leaves on its stem. The froghopper jumps 2 inches down to reach the nearest leaf. Then it jumps another 3 inches down to reach another leaf. Then, it jumps to the next leaf, which is 3 more inches down. How far above the ground is the froghopper now?

14 inches - 2 inches - 3 inches - 3 inches = 6 inches

> This number line will help you subtract. Start at the 14-inch mark and take away 2, which brings you to 12. Then, take away 3 to reach 9. Finally, take away 3 more inches. That means the froghopper is 6 inches above the ground.

15
14
13 — first leaf
12
11
10 — second leaf
9
8
7 — third leaf
6
5
4
3
2
1
0
inches

11

The flea is another good jumper. It can jump as far as 33 centimeters and as high as 18 centimeters.

Fleas and froghoppers can jump really far. Imagine that a froghopper jumps 14 centimeters and a flea jumps 9 centimeters. How can you use a number line to add and subtract these numbers?

```
  14 centimeters          14 centimeters
+  9 centimeters        -  9 centimeters
  ─────────────           ─────────────
  23 centimeters           5 centimeters
```

The first number line shows the sum of the numbers when you add them. The second number line shows the **difference** between the numbers when you subtract them.

flea

froghopper

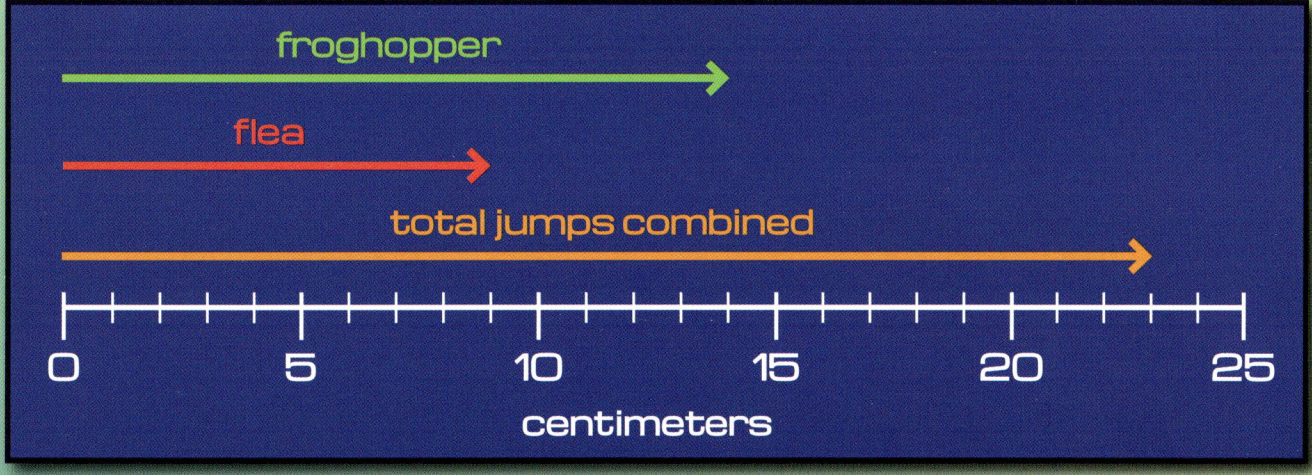

froghopper

flea

total jumps combined

0 5 10 15 20 25
centimeters

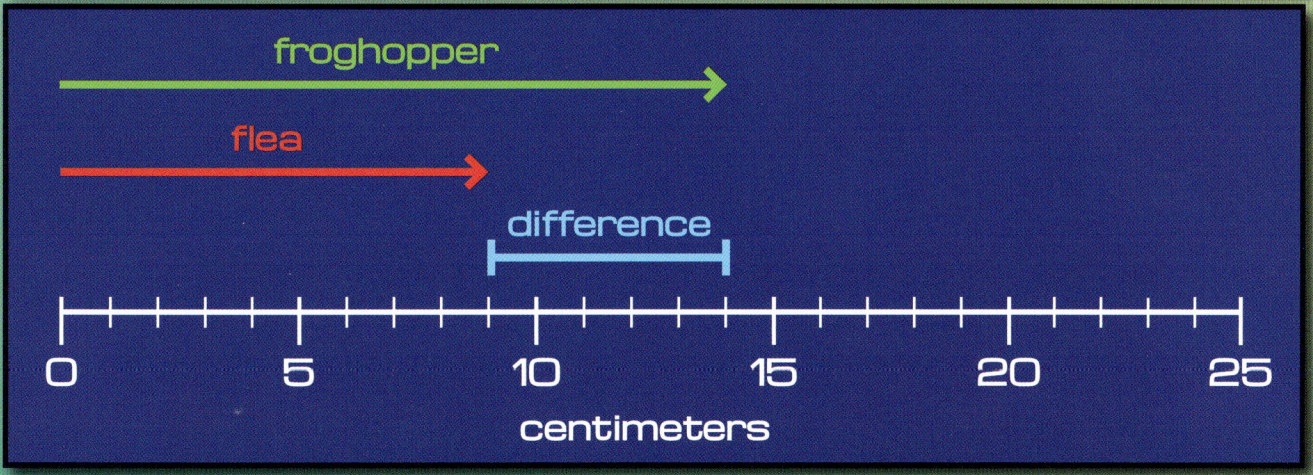

froghopper

flea

difference

0 5 10 15 20 25
centimeters

Jumping Cats

All kinds of cats jump—from your pet cat to big cats in the jungle. One of the best jumpers is the snow leopard. These beautiful animals can jump as far as 50 feet (15 m)!

Imagine that a snow leopard sees prey that's 90 feet away. It makes a 40-foot jump first, then a 25-foot jump. How many feet are left between the snow leopard and its prey?

> This number line shows the snow leopard jumps a total of 90 feet. The number line also shows the first 2 jumps are 65 feet altogether. Count the marks between 65 and 90 to learn the length of the third jump. It's 25 feet!

40 feet
25 feet
+ ?? feet
―――――
90 feet

first jump   second jump   third jump

0 5 10 15 20 25 30 35 40 45 50 55 60 65 70 75 80 85 90 95 100
feet

15

A number line can help you compare the snow leopard's jumps. Drawing a line for each jump shows the differences between them.

Make a number line that goes from 1 to 50. Each number stands for a foot. The numbers should be equally spaced. Draw the first line from 0 to 40. Draw a second line from 0 to 25. Then, draw a third line from 0 to 25. What do you notice?

> Use this number line to help you understand the snow leopard's jumps. For example, the longest line shows the longest jump. What else can you tell by looking at the number line?

first jump

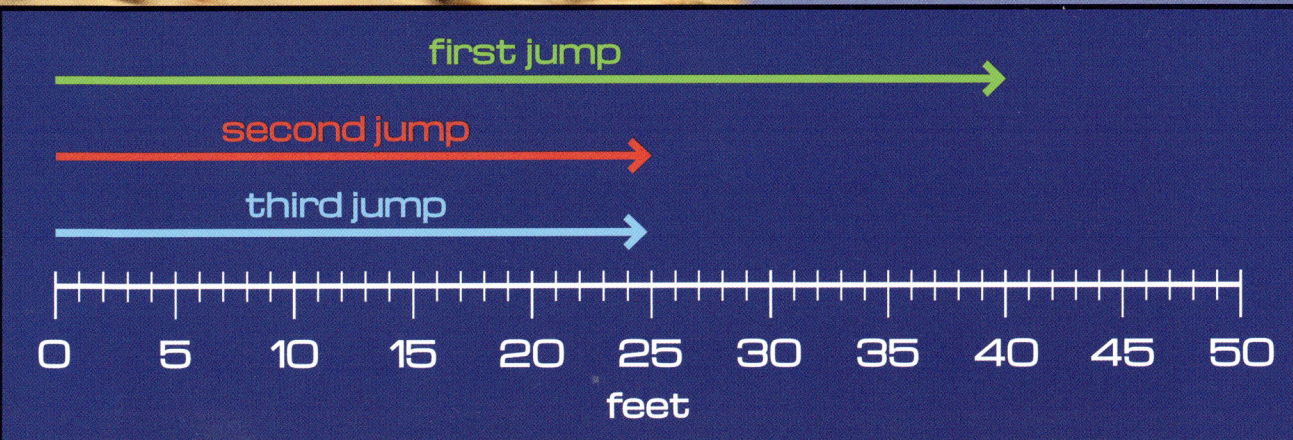

second jump

third jump

feet

Who Else Jumps?

The hare is another animal that jumps a lot. A hare moves by jumping quickly across grass and snow.

Imagine that a hare jumps 39 meters in 1 day. It jumps 22 meters in the morning and 17 meters in the afternoon. How many more meters did it jump in the morning? Try using a number line to help you solve this problem.

> This number line shows the total distance jumped by the hare, as well as how much it jumped in the morning and afternoon. Look at the difference between the morning line and the afternoon line. The green line is 5 marks longer than the red line. So, the hare jumped 5 more meters in the morning.

morning
afternoon
total

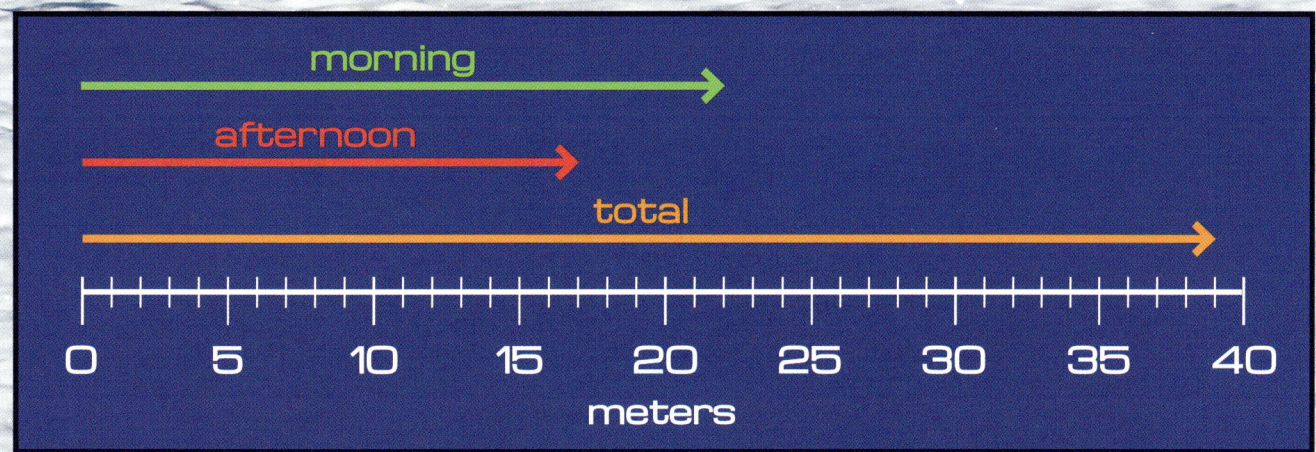

meters

Have you heard of kangaroos? They jump, too. Adult kangaroos have longer jumps than baby kangaroos.

Imagine an adult kangaroo and a baby kangaroo both jump 10 feet. The baby kangaroo makes 5 jumps that are 2 feet each. The adult kangaroo makes 2 jumps that are 5 feet each. Use a number line to show how their jumps are different.

> Although the adult and baby kangaroo jumped the same distance, the baby kangaroo's jumps are smaller. How does the number line show this?

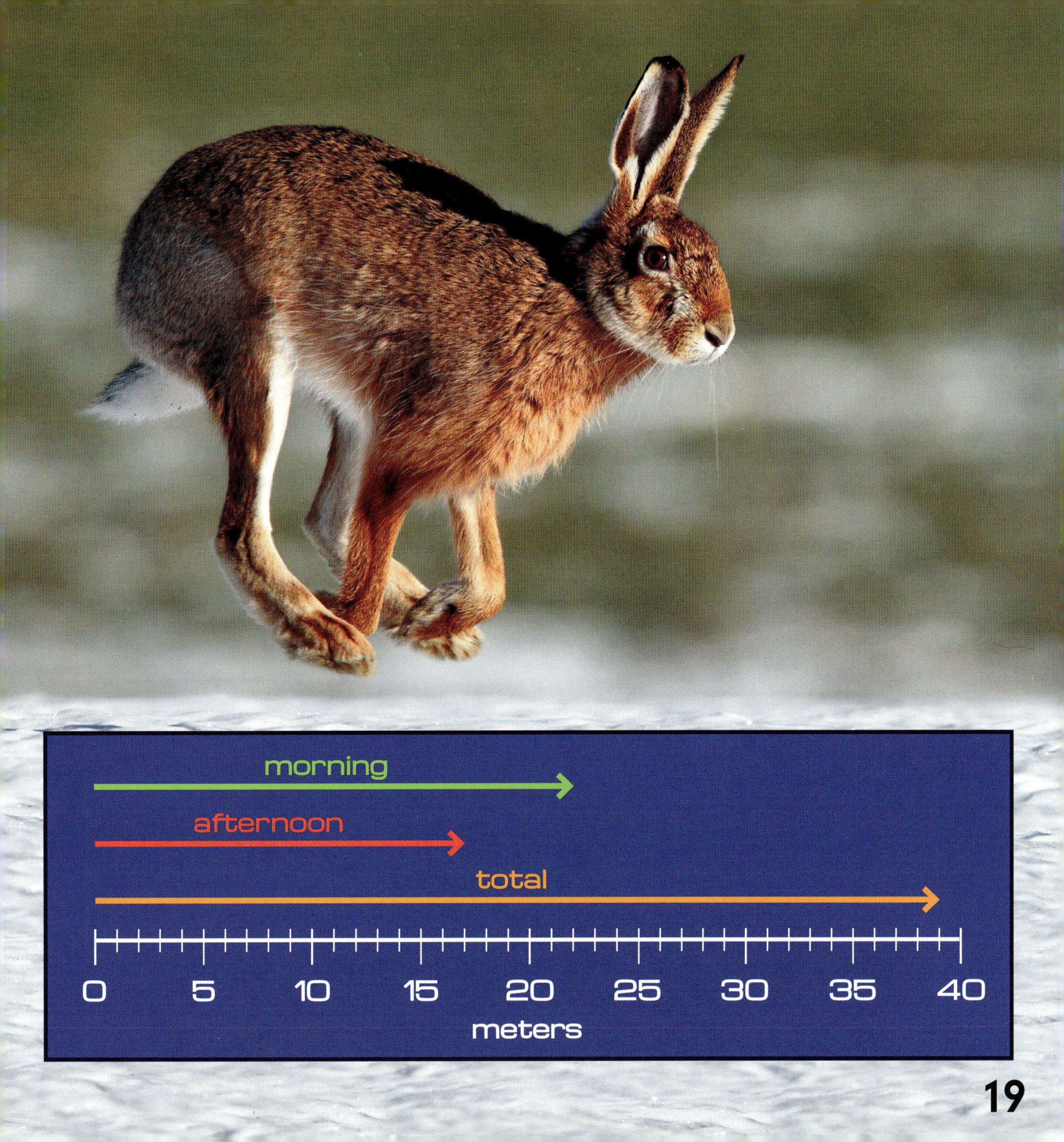
morning
afternoon
total
0
5
10
15
20
25
30
35
40
meters

Have you heard of kangaroos? They jump, too. Adult kangaroos have longer jumps than baby kangaroos.

Imagine an adult kangaroo and a baby kangaroo both jump 10 feet. The baby kangaroo makes 5 jumps that are 2 feet each. The adult kangaroo makes 2 jumps that are 5 feet each. Use a number line to show how their jumps are different.

> Although the adult and baby kangaroo jumped the same distance, the baby kangaroo's jumps are smaller. How does the number line show this?

10 feet – baby kangaroo

10 feet – adult kangaroo

0 1 2 3 4 5 6 7 8 9 10
feet

21

Measuring Movements

It's fun to learn about animals that jump. It's even more fun when you use a number line to record the length of their jumps. You can use number lines to show more than just animal's jumps, though. They can show how far animals swim, how fast they run, or any other facts you'd like to show!

Glossary

adapt (uh-DAPT) To change to fit new conditions.

difference (DIH-fuh-ruhns) The amount that is left after subtracting numbers.

distance (DIHS-tuhns) The amount of space between two things.

environment (ihn-VY-ruhn-muhnt) The natural world around us.

unit (YOO-nuht) A standard amount by which things are measured.

Index

centimeters, 6, 12, 13

compare, 16

difference, 12, 16, 18

feet, 6, 14, 15, 16, 17, 20, 21

flea, 12, 13

froghopper, 8, 10, 12, 13

hare, 18

inches, 6, 7, 8, 9, 10, 11

kangaroos, 20, 21

meters, 6, 18, 19

snow leopard, 14, 16

sum, 12